I Love Castles

By Lisa Regan
Illustrated by Graham Sumner

First published in 2009 by Miles Kelly Publishing Ltd
Bardfield Centre, Great Bardfield, Essex, CM7 4SL

Copyright © Miles Kelly Publishing Ltd 2009

2 4 6 8 10 9 7 5 3 1

Editorial Director Belinda Gallagher
Art Director Jo Brewer
Senior Editor Rosie McGuire
Editorial Assistant Toby Tippen
Designers Graham Sumner, Jo Brewer
Cover Artworker Carmen Johnson
Production Manager Elizabeth Brunwin
Reprographics Ian Paulyn, Stephan Davis
Archive Manager Jennifer Hunt

ISBN 978-1-84810-044-2

Printed in Thailand

All images are from the Miles Kelly Archives

British Library Cataloguing-in-Publication Data
A catalogue record for this book is available
from the British Library

Made with paper from a sustainable forest

www.mileskelly.net   info@mileskelly.net

www.factsforprojects.com

Contents

Building a castle

Around 700 years ago, castles were built of stone. Stone was a good material because it was strong, and could not be burnt down by an enemy. A single castle would take many hundreds of workers years to build.

The master mason was in charge of the workers. He followed the orders of the lord who was going to live in the castle.

The heaviest materials were placed in buckets and hauled up using ropes and pulleys to where they were needed.

Workers carried stones, dug trenches and mixed mortar (sand and water), which was used to fill gaps between stones.

Tools

There were no electric tools 700 years ago – everything was made by hand. Carpenters used axes, saws and handsaws.

In the kitchen

Kitchen servants prepared meals every day and banquets (feasts) for special occasions. Everybody had a different job to do. The kitchen was hot and smoky, with a roaring fire all year round.

Cooks peeled and chopped vegetables, and plucked and carved meat.

Storage
Special wines and cooking oils were stored in large clay pots.

There were no fridges, so meat was preserved using salt or smoke. Cooks added lots of spices to hide the taste of food that had gone bad!

Every castle kitchen had a cauldron (a big iron pot). These were hung over the open fire to cook meat and vegetables.

Meat was cooked over the fire on a spit (pole). A servant known as a 'turnspit' turned the pole slowly so that the meat cooked evenly.

Time for a feast

Banquets (feasts) were served in the great hall on special occasions. The lord and his most important guests sat at the high table, on a raised platform above the other guests.

Special guests had gold or silver plates, but everyone else ate off trenchers (thick slices of bread).

People used knives to cut up their food. Then they used spoons or their fingers to eat it – there were no forks!

Important guests were given the best food. This could include wild boar, beef, duck, swan or peacock.

Musicians provided entertainment, playing instruments such as rebecs, which were similar to modern violins.

Fine wines

Servants called cup-bearers poured wine from decorated pottery jugs into wine glasses.

The solar

The lord and his family had a private living area known as the solar. This room, or set of rooms, was where the family could sleep or spend their free time. The solar was peaceful and quiet, away from the noise and bustle of the rest of the castle.

Long curtains hanging around beds could be pulled shut to keep in warmth.

Growing up

After the age of seven, the son of a nobleman might be sent to live in another lord's castle, where he would be trained to become a knight.

Servants played instruments such as harps. The lord's children were taught to sing and dance.

The chapel

The most beautiful room in a castle was the chapel. The lord and his family attended a service there at least once every day. The lord would also visit the priest with his knights to ask for God's blessing and protection in battle.

Tapestries, paintings and stained-glass windows illustrated religious scenes and stories.

A server assisted the priest. He carried a censer (small dish), containing burning incense, which let off sweet-smelling smoke.

No one worked on holy days. Everyone in the castle celebrated religious festivals such as Easter.

Priests performed religious ceremonies, such as blessing the lord and lady.

Pilgrimage
Religion was very important. People went on long pilgrimages (journeys to visit holy places) to prove that their faith was strong.

Falconry

Another popular pastime was falconry. A servant called a falconer trained birds of prey, such as falcons, to hunt for rabbits and small birds. Training the birds took time and great skill.

A hood was placed over the bird's head to keep it calm until it was released to fly.

Birds of prey

Falconers didn't just train falcons. Other birds of prey used in falconry included hawks, eagles and buzzards.

A thick leather glove protected the falconer's arm from the bird's sharp claws.

Birds were trained to fly back to the person that released them.

Both lords and ladies took part in falconry. Ladies rode side-saddle (sat sideways on their horses) because of their long skirts.

Jousting

Tournaments (mock battles) were put on for entertainment. One event was the joust, in which two knights tried to knock each other off their horses using lances (long spears). The loser had to pay the winner money, or give him his horse or armour.

A wooden rail separated the two riders. If one knight fell the rail stopped him being trodden on by the other knight's horse.

Knights aimed to hit their opponent's head, chest or shield with their lance.

The lances had to be equal in length to make the contest fair.

Well-wishers

Jousts were watched by everyone, including ladies of the court. A lady might give her favourite knight a scarf for good luck.

Jousts weren't usually fights to the death. Lances had metal tips, but these were often blunt (not sharp).

Arming a knight

Knights wore metal armour for protection in battle, but without care it could get rusty or broken. Armour was stored in a room called the armoury, and was mended and cleaned by the armourer and his workmen. It could take an hour to dress a knight for battle.

Coats of arms (special badges) on shields helped knights to recognize each other in battle.

Knights wore armoured gloves known as gauntlets. These were made of leather, with steel plates stitched to the outside.

Armour made of metal plates gave the best protection.

Knights were dressed by pages or squires. Armour was put on from the feet upwards.

Chain mail

Armourers made rings of steel and linked them to create 'chain mail'. This type of armour was flexible and tough.

Into battle

Battles were fought to end disagreements or to gain land, wealth and power. Knights and soldiers fought for the lord who looked after them or gave them land. Soldiers marched or rode into battle, carrying the flag and coat of arms (badge) of their lord.

Armour everywhere

Even horses wore armour! Men with armoured horses were put in the front rank (row) during battle.

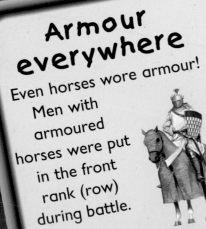

The drawbridge could be pulled up to stop enemies crossing the moat below.

Ordinary soldiers fought on foot. They were usually townspeople, brought in to help if there was a war.

Under attack

Attacking enemies had to break through a castle's defences to get inside its walls. If an enemy surrounded a castle, trapping the people inside, it was called a siege. If no help came, the people inside would run out of food or other supplies, and have to surrender (admit defeat).

Huge siege weapons were used to fling stones at the castle walls to weaken them.

Soldiers fired arrows at the people in the castle. They stood behind mantlets (giant wooden shields) for protection.

Battlements along the tops of the walls gave the soldiers inside the castle something to hide behind.

Attacking armies sometimes tunnelled under the castle walls to get inside.

At the gates
Attackers could try to break down the castle gates with giant battering rams (wooden beams with metal heads).

Fun facts

Building a castle Castles had narrow slits instead of windows so archers could fire arrows through the slits without being hit by the enemy.

In the kitchen The cook didn't add salt during cooking. Diners added their own salt from a bowl shaped like a ship.

Time for a feast Honey was added to food and drink to make it sweet. It was also used to make an alcoholic drink called mead.

The solar Some castles had a private toilet (garderobe) next to the solar. Waste went into a special pit or into the moat!

The chapel Large castles might have had more than one chapel. The lord had his own private chapel and everyone else used a larger chapel.

Falconry The type of bird you used depended on your status. A king had a gyr falcon. Lords had peregrine falcons.

Jousting Other tournament events included pretend battles, sword fights, wrestling and archery competitions.

Arming a knight It was difficult to walk wearing armour, because it was very heavy. It was designed to be worn when riding a horse.

Into battle When the soldiers left the castle, a huge portcullis (heavy iron gate) slid down to block the entrance.

Under attack A siege tower was a large wooden tower on wheels. Armies pushed siege towers against the castle walls so soldiers could climb up them and attack.